Finns

IN WISCONSIN

Revised and Expanded Edition

Mark Knipping

WISCONSIN HISTORICAL SOCIETY PRESS

9.45
6-10

Published by the Wisconsin Historical Society Press
Publishers since 1855

© 2008 by the State Historical Society of Wisconsin

For permission to reuse material from *Finns in Wisconsin*, revised
and expanded edition, (ISBN 978-0-87020-390-9), please access
www.copyright.com or contact the Copyright Clearance Center, Inc.
(CCC), 222 Rosewood Drive, Danvers, MA 01923, 978-750-8400.
CCC is a not-for-profit organization that provides
licenses and registration for a variety of users.

www.wisconsinhistory.org

Photographs identified with WHi are from the Society's collections;
address inquiries about such photos to the
Visual Materials Archivist at Wisconsin Historical Society,
816 State Street, Madison, WI 53706.

The excerpt of "From Köyhäjoki Kaustinen To Florida"
is reprinted with permission of the Lutheran Church-Missouri Synod.

Printed in Wisconsin, U.S.A.

Designed by Jane Tenenbaum

12 11 10 09 08   1 2 3 4 5

Library of Congress Cataloging-in-Publication Data
Knipping, Mark H.
Finns in Wisconsin / Mark Knipping. — Rev. and expanded ed.
p. cm.
Includes bibliographical references and index.
ISBN 978-0-87020-390-9 (pbk. : alk. paper)
1. Finnish Americans — Wisconsin — History. 2. Wisconsin — History.
I. Title.
F590.F5K5 2008
977.5'00494541—dc22

2008001316

♾ The paper used in this publication meets the minimum requirements
of the American National Standard for Information Sciences —
Permanence of Paper for Printed Library Materials, ANSI Z39.48–1992.

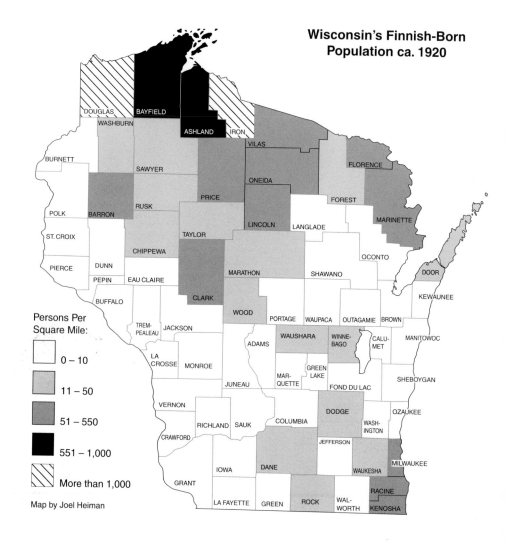

Wisconsin's Finnish-Born Population ca. 1920

DOUGLAS
BAYFIELD
WASHBURN
ASHLAND
IRON
VILAS
BURNETT
SAWYER
ONEIDA
FLORENCE
PRICE
FOREST
POLK
RUSK
LINCOLN
MARINETTE
BARRON
LANGLADE
ST. CROIX
TAYLOR
CHIPPEWA
OCONTO
PIERCE
DUNN
MARATHON
SHAWANO
DOOR
PEPIN
EAU CLAIRE
KEWAUNEE
BUFFALO
CLARK
WOOD
TREM-
PEALEAU
JACKSON
PORTAGE
WAUPACA
OUTAGAMIE
BROWN
WAUSHARA
WINNE-
BAGO
CALU-
MET
MANITOWOC
ADAMS
LA
CROSSE
MONROE
GREEN
LAKE
MAR-
QUETTE
JUNEAU
FOND DU LAC
SHEBOYGAN
VERNON
DODGE
OZAUKEE
RICHLAND
SAUK
COLUMBIA
WASH-
INGTON
CRAWFORD
JEFFERSON
MILWAUKEE
IOWA
DANE
WAUKESHA
GRANT
RACINE
LA FAYETTE
GREEN
ROCK
WAL-
WORTH
KENOSHA

Persons Per
Square Mile:

0 – 10

11 – 50

51 – 550

551 – 1,000

More than 1,000

Map by Joel Heiman

EARLY FINNISH IMMIGRATION

Between 1864 and 1920 more than 300,000 Finns left Suomi, the name they gave to Finland in their native tongue. Most of them were bound for the United States, where they hoped to find the freedoms and opportunities denied them in their homeland. Despite the fact that they were relatively late additions to the mass migrations from western Europe and Scandinavia, not reaching Wisconsin in sizable numbers until the late 1880s, they were not newcomers to the immigrant scene. Historically, Finns had been among the earliest ethnic groups to help colonize America. In 1683 William Penn, proprietary governor of the colony he had established in Pennsylvania, wrote: "The first planters in these parts were the Dutch, and soon after the Sweeds and Finns. The Dutch applied themselves to Traffick, the Sweeds and Finns to husbandry."

In that same year another Englishman commented on the Finnish settlers' preference for rye bread, their homespun linen clothing, and in particular on their style of domestic architecture in which they "use but little Iron... for they will build and hardly use any other toole but an Ax." Although by the 1700s the Pennsylvania Finns had been indistinguishably absorbed into the neighboring English and German-speaking communities, they left one enduring legacy — the pioneer log cabin — and in succeeding generations the Scandinavian log house would become symbolic of the expanding American frontier.

Finland has always been a vast, empty land of short growing seasons and long, hard winters. The landscape is varied, from the flat plains of Bothnia to the frozen mountains of Lapland. The countryside is dotted with some 66,000 shimmering lakes and blanketed with dense forests of pine, fir, and birch.

Into this largely uncultivatable region the ancestors of the Finns began infiltrating about AD 100, gradually pushing the native nomadic Lapps northward. By the middle of the ninth century Finnish settlement had advanced northeast to Karelia, and the various invading tribes had formed themselves into three unities: the Finns, the Tavastians, and the Karelians. Caught between their two more powerful and aggressive neighbors, Sweden and Russia, it was centuries before a true Finnish state could emerge. Sweden annexed the Tavastian territory in the thirteenth century, divided Karelia with Russia in 1323, and began settling the Finnish shoreline. Swedish became the language of administrative officials and the upper classes who maintained little contact with the common Finnish people.

A long series of wars between the Swedes and the Russians resulted in minor border changes throughout the eighteenth century, until in 1808 Czar Alexander I invaded Finland to thwart Sweden's pro-British policies. In the following year Finland was formally annexed as a Grand Duchy of Russia, thus setting the stage for an out-migration which would continue for over a century. Under Czarist rule, adventurous Finns began leaving for the North American Continent where they made up an important segment of the work force in the Russian fur-trading colonies in Alaska. Indeed, in 1840 it is estimated that between 200 and 250 Finns were employed as sailors and shipbuilders in the capital city of Sitka alone; but these ventures, attracting mainly young, single men, were limited in scope and duration and did little to promote permanent settlement.

The first large-scale Finnish migration to the United States began in the 1860s and was composed of Finns who had abandoned the poor northern province of Oulu to seek work as miners, fishermen, and small farmers in neighboring Norway's Finmark and Tromso provinces. But life in Norway proved as unendurably harsh as it had been in Finland; farmers fought despairing battles against the thin, stony soil, crippling icy winds, and short growing seasons; many fishermen never returned from storm-tossed seas, leading to the common saying that "Few of the poor fishermen end their days in bed." America beckoned ever more strongly, and while the total number of Finnish emigrants from artic Norway and Russian Finland to the U.S. probably did not exceed 1,000 persons from 1863 to 1885, their early efforts demonstrated to their countrymen that it was possible to escape the oppressive conditions at home for fresh opportunities in the New World. Most of these early migrants eventually settled in the mining areas of the Upper Peninsula of Michigan, drawn there through the efforts of the Mining Emigrant Association, whose agents solicited workers in Canada, Norway, and Sweden.

ECONOMIC AND SOCIAL CHANGES

Beginning in the middle of the nineteenth century, dramatic economic and social changes brought new pressures to bear upon the Finnish people. For centuries Finland had existed as an agrarian economy with a traditional, immobile society. Because of the harsh climate and rugged terrain, farmers were able to cultivate less than ten percent of the country's land surface, primarily growing grain crops such as rye, oats, and wheat that required a large labor supply during harvest time. The rural population was mainly composed of farm laborers and tenant farmers working for the wealthy, landed classes, accustomed to a barter system in which goods and services were traded for the few items needed on the independent estates beyond what could be produced locally. Immense stands of timber provided the raw material for building construction, carts and sledges, furniture, eating utensils, tools, and articles of amusement. Indigenous raw materials for textiles included wool, flax, and, to a lesser extent, hemp. In early times, iron was made from bog ore (a brown ore found in swampy areas), and later could be had by barter.

The traditional self-sufficient farm units were small in size, owing to the fact that beginning about 1750, the state took steps to combine scattered landholdings into larger, more efficient farming units. These changes displaced many of the small farmers, who were reduced to working as farm laborers or tenant farmers, or who simply became vagabonds in search of their next meal. The disappearance of small, independent farmers continued into the twentieth century: in 1901, forty-three percent of all rural households were those of landless farm laborers, while another thirty-four percent toiled as tenant farmers. Only twenty-three percent owned their own land. Moreover, about seventy percent of all farms totaled less than twenty acres of cultivated land, and over thirty percent of all farms were smaller than five acres. In addition to paying his landlord a cash rent, tenants were often obliged to spend a specified number of "foot days" and "horse days" each year, laboring on the landowner's acreage.

Beginning in the 1860s, a great many economic and social changes began to erode the old order. Agriculture shifted away from cereal crops toward dairying, so that grass, which required a minimal number of farm laborers, replaced grain as the primary crop. This change, along with the introduction of labor-saving farm machinery such as hay mowers, had the effect of releasing many farm laborers from the agricultural work force to join the army of homeless workers searching for employment. The creation of an ever-growing landless class in turn stimulated a money economy in which hard cash was exchanged for goods and services. Agriculture was transformed from a subsistence labor-intensive system into a capitalistic market economy in which alternate crops, requiring large farm machinery and fewer farm workers, put thousands of workers into the landless, jobless category.

The old barter system fell into disuse, and with it went much of the folk culture of Finland. The new money economy and profit motive broke down the traditional self-sufficient farm unit, and cash sale replaced home consumption, setting large numbers of Finns adrift in their own land. Prince Peter Kropotkin was a revolutionary Russian nobleman who was later imprisoned because of his social beliefs. While studying in Finland he wrote of the Finnish farmers' wretched lot in 1899: "What is the use of talking to this peasant about American machines, when he has barely enough bread to live upon from one crop to the next; when the rent which he has to pay for that boulder-clay grows heavier and heavier in proportion to his success in improving the soil? He gnaws at his hard-as-a-stone rye flour cake which he bakes twice a year; he has with it a morsel of fearfully salted cod and a drink of skimmed milk. How dare I talk to him of American machines, when all that he can raise must be sold to pay rent and taxes?"

Time-honored traditions created further family hardships. The Finns still observed the ancient system of primogeniture, in which the eldest son inherited the family farm, while all other sons joined the ranks of the landless poor. While the practice was necessary from the standpoint of preventing the already small farms from being divided among several sons with each passing generation, it also caused social dislocations, since the family farm was preserved at the cost of the younger sons. A Finnish American worker wrote: "As the son of a small landowner, I enjoyed bread and warmth at home until my eldest brother became master of the farm. From that time on, home no longer felt like home, and the prospect of becoming a hired hand in my own community was not attractive. There was no way by which I could become a landowner, and I knew no vocation save that of a farmer. So, to America!"

Parallel changes were also taking place in Finland's various extractive industries, such as logging and mining. An Imperial Decree in 1861 lifted many of the old restrictions on the lumbering industry, and unemployed farmers abandoned the plow for the axe, following the forests' retreat inland. The end of the Franco-Prussian War in 1871 signaled an even greater demand for lumber, further stimulating the industry. Railroad construction boomed at the same time, as logging operations pushed into the country's interior. A large rootless class of laborers, recruited primarily from the landless agricultural workers, moved restlessly over the countryside in search of employment in these seasonal industries.

Factory workers in the cities also faced uncertain futures, slaving long hours for low wages and subject to frequent unemployment and hazardous working conditions. The enormous surplus of workers kept wages low, and the children of working families were compelled to toil in factories from an early age onward. August Tornquist, who later emigrated to Kenosha, wrote of his boyhood in Finland: "At the age of nine, I worked in a tobacco factory from six in the morning until eight at night; at the age of ten, I was pasting labels in a brewery; at eleven, I was a shoemaker's helper; at thirteen, a tinsmith's boy; at fourteen, a shoemaker's apprentice — these were my childhood games, these were my childhood joys." During the winter of 1892 almost three-fourths of Helsinki's workers were unemployed. There was famine during that year and the next, and in 1894 there were bread riots. Starvation was nothing new to the Finns. The country's population more than tripled during the nineteenth century, and food production was subject to the whims of a harsh climate. Adverse weather caused a series of crop failures, and severe famine swept the land from 1862 till 1868. During one three-year period in the 1860s there were 107,000 more deaths than births. In 1868, when starvation reached its peak, one parish recorded thirty-one births and 765 deaths. One out of thirteen Finns died that year. The years 1892–1893 and 1903 also saw widespread hunger, deprivation, and starvation, though not as severe as the decade of the 1860s. In 1905, an eighty-nine-year-old woman recalled the famine years: "The bark of the pine tree was mixed with ground straw, but good God it was bitter and tough. I could not swallow a mouthful; I spit it out, for my heart could not accept it."

To add to the Finns' grief, compulsory military service was forced upon the male population in 1878, with the result that many young men left the country to avoid the draft. The situation worsened in 1901, when Russia ordered the Finnish army to disband and incorporated the Finnish soldiers into the Czarist army. Wholesale noncompliance resulted, with many young men refusing to report for induction, and many others leaving for the United States to escape military service.

A rigid class structure, in which a few persons owned and controlled most of the country's assets, left the mass of the population without a voice in governmental affairs. At the end of the nineteenth century, only 6.7 percent of the urban residents and 4.3 percent of the rural inhabitants could vote in national elections. The upper classes resisted all changes to better the lot of the working poor, opposing reform as well as out-migration, which they feared would reduce manpower and thereby raise wages and labor's demands. Suffering from overpopulation, periodic mass unemployment and occasional mass starvation, plagued with an upper class interested only in maintaining its power while remaining unconcerned with the well-being of general population, and faced with the constant menace of the Great Russian Bear growling from the East, Finns nevertheless clung to a dream of personal independence. One of their proverbs aptly summed up the Finnish spirit: "Oma tupa, oma lupa" — "One's own home, one's own master." It was a dream they knew could never come true in their homeland; perhaps in America it could. Accordingly, between 1864 and 1920, more than 300,000 Finns chose the westward route across the Atlantic, leaving everything behind — roots, families, careers and memories, knowing in their hearts they could never return. Most of them were bound for the United States.

THE VOYAGE TO AMERICA

The Finnish Steamship Company, founded in 1883, had been granted a monopoly to sell transatlantic steamship passage to Finnish travelers. For most, the price of a ticket to America was expensive, though it cost only 150 Finnish marks (about thirty-six dollars) to journey from Finland to New York in 1890. Roughly one-third of the travelers drew upon their own savings, another third borrowed the fare from banks or individuals, while the final third received help in the form of tickets or money from friends and relatives in America.

Between 1880 and 1920, out of every hundred Finnish emigrants, forty-eight came from the province of Vaasa, sixteen from Turku-Pori, fifteen from Oulu, seven from Viipuri, five from Uusimaa, four from Kuopio, three from Hame, and two from Mikkeli. They usually departed from the seaport of Hanko, near Helsinki, sometimes seven hundred of them crowding into town at a time, some wearing Pori fur hats, some shod in boots with turned-up toes, some with curved pipes clenched between their teeth. The port's few inns provided inadequate accommodations, and most were compelled to sleep on the hostel's wooden floors. During the daytime they walked the city streets, taking in the new and exciting sights of urban life. They checked and rechecked their precious tickets, rearranged the contents of their red-painted trunks, nibbled at rye bread, herring, and cheese. Sailing schedules were irregular and oftentimes they had to wait for several days before they could depart, exhausting their meager food supplies.

On sailing day they carried their few possessions to dockside, where they were roughly herded aboard ship. An English observer wrote of the departure of these travelers: "I have a moment of intense regret when I think of the crowd of exiles collected like sheep at the emigration offices, and marched in a straggling line to the boat where passports, tickets, and goods were examined as though they belonged to beasts... [and] that the cargoes of butter in wooden casks received better handling and accommodations than the human freight."

The ships bore fine names, such as *Urania, Sirius, Polaris, Arcturus*, and *Titania*, but smelled far from heavenly. The *Arcturus* usually carried nearly five hundred third-class passengers per trip, packing them into filthy compartments belowdecks — men and women, young and old, sick and dying among the healthy.

It was three and one-half days by ship from Hanko to the English port of Hull, where the emigrants then boarded a train to Liverpool or Southampton. There were more sights to be seen as they gazed out of the coach windows at sooty factory towns separated by open green meadows. They rolled onward to the port cities in a holiday mood, shouting an exuberant "Gut-bai" to somewhat startled Britishers, who politely doffed their caps and waved a reply to the speeding train. Once in the port cities, the emigrants lodged in cheap dockside hotels for a few days before taking passage to America. They boarded ships of lines such as Allan, Cunard, American, or White Star for the Atlantic Crossing to New York, Boston, Montreal, or Quebec.

Upon arriving in the States, Finnish immigrants usually struck out for communities dominated by some major industry, or for the mines and lumber camps, which needed large numbers of unskilled laborers. Most of the arrivals came from the landless or small landowning classes, including agricultural laborers, tenant farmers, small landowners, and the children of small landowners. They were described as "stiff-necked, endowed with the strength of a bear and the endurance of a mule," and were disciplined to perform even the most dismal jobs. Since about eighty-five percent of them were rural peasants, and only fifteen percent came from the cities, they entered the American labor market on the bottom rung of the employment ladder as low-paid, unskilled laborers. During the first decade of the twentieth century American immigration officials classified over sixty percent of the Finnish men as general laborers — one of the highest percentages among all immigrant groups.

SETTLING IN WISCONSIN

Finnish immigration to Wisconsin actually began in a serious way during the late 1880s, and that they would settle in northern Wisconsin was almost inevitable, situated as it was between Michigan and Minnesota, states ranking first and second respectively in their foreign-born Finnish populations. Although the landscape of the Wisconsin area resembled Finland, economic opportunity was by far the most important factor influencing Finnish settlement patterns in the Western Great Lakes region. For this reason the state, with its limited mining, never attracted the numbers of Finns as did Michigan and Minnesota. By 1900 there were 2,198 Finns in Wisconsin, a number which increased to 5,705 by 1910. The figure for 1920 was 6,757, but by 1930 it declined to 5,724, and had fallen to 4,715 in 1940. The Finns were not widely dispersed: three counties (Douglas, Iron, and Bayfield) accounted for more than one-half, and these, together with Price and Ashland, for two-thirds of Wisconsin's total Finnish population for the period after 1910.

The goal of many arriving Finns was to establish themselves as small independent farmers. Agriculture had been their experience in Finland, and the hearty life of farming, coupled with a little wintertime logging, held great appeal for them. A few families filed for homestead claims upon arrival in Wisconsin, and proceeded to hack a living out of the wilderness. But though the Finns often dreamed of a small farm as their escape from a wage-earner's life of toil, their poverty upon arrival dictated some delay. Significantly, between 1890 and 1910, most were forced to take temporary jobs as laborers in order to save enough to purchase a farm. They found work in the copper and iron mines, in factories, and on the railroad. Some tried fishing or sailing, and others labored as dockhands. Most of the Wisconsin Finns tried logging at some time or other, and many who later turned to farming continued to work in the woods to provide wintertime income.

Mining probably ranked first on a national basis in absorbing Finnish workers, and thousands went almost directly from the trains into the mine shafts. They dug copper ore in Upper Michigan and iron ore in Minnesota's Mesabi Range and Wisconsin's Iron and Marinette counties. The first Finns began to arrive at Montreal in Iron County in 1887, where they labored as trammers, filling and pushing loaded ore cars through the mine shafts. The cities of Hurley and Iron Belt boomed as Finnish miners crowded into the boardinghouses, and made their daily 4,000-foot descent to wrest low-grade iron ore from the earth. Mining was hard and dangerous: rockfalls, undependable blasting powder, smoldering fires, choking dust, and poison gas exacted their toll. There were 146 fatal mining accidents in a single Upper Michigan county between 1900 and 1903.

Wisconsin quarries also drew a share of Finnish workers. Stonecutters settled at Amberg in Marinette County and at Redgranite in Waushara County. Quarried red granite was then in vogue for construction of public buildings, as well as for paving stones to be laid in Milwaukee and Chicago. The village of Amberg was described during its heyday as "lit up like a city at night." Seven saloons provided liquor and companionship to hundreds of loggers, railroad workers, and quarrymen, requiring a full-time constable to patrol the rowdy streets after dark.

Railroads offered employment to Finns, who were especially numerous in the section gangs of the Duluth, South Shore and Atlantic line, the Duluth, Mesabi and Iron Range road, and the Northern Pacific railroad. Finnish workers were sought out as "a hardy set of men, steady of purpose and habit, frugal, sober and industrious." A Duluth railroad agent placed an advertisement in several Finnish American newspapers in 1905: "500 Finnish railroad men wanted. $2.25 a day. Board costs $4.00 a week. Pay every 20th day of the month and moreover it can be obtained whenever wanted. 8 new living quarters. All letters answered in Finnish."

Factories in Milwaukee hired Finnish machinists as well as general laborers. In Racine and Kenosha they primarily found employment in tanneries, though conditions there were not to their liking. A Racine Finn described the work as "heavy, dirty, and bloody," and not at all as he had known the trade in Oulu. The pace of American factories was altogether new to these peasant workers, who liked to pause now and then for a smoke, a cup of coffee, or a friendly word. Even those who had labored in factories in Finland found the pace faster here, and the conditions dark, dirty, and dangerous. Many Finnish workers became active in the American labor movement as socialists, communists, and members of the Industrial Workers of the World — the famed IWW — which primarily organized mining, lumbering, and agricultural laborers before World War I. Their radical approach to labor organization mirrored the Finns' low social station, as well as their cultural heritage: the Labour Party was founded in Finland in 1899, and adopted Marxist tenets in 1903, developing along revolutionary lines. Their position on the bottom rung of the employment ladder made it necessary to organize unions in order to secure a living wage, for a family simply could not live on the wages offered immigrants. (In a South Superior chair factory during the 1890s Finnish workers earned seventy-five cents for a ten-hour working day.) Lake Superior provided numerous Finns with employment. Some found work as sailors, though their number was not very large. They could be recognized by their colorful tattoos, whose cheerful effect belied their actual purpose of aiding in identifying a drowned sailor.

Fishermen also took to the lake, rowing their small boats out from Wisconsin port villages such as Herbster, Cornucopia, and Port Wing. They set and pulled in their nets by hand, rowing for an entire day in open wooden boats. Arriving home after dark, they hand-cleaned their catch by the flickering light of a lantern. They often worked sixteen hours a day when weather allowed, and sewed or mended nets when winter's wind made fishing impossible. Finns also worked at dockside on the Great Lakes, loading ore boats in Marquette, Michigan; Duluth, Minnesota; and Ashland and Superior, Wisconsin. Gangs of Finns in turn unloaded these same ships at their destinations in Cleveland, Fairport, Ashtabula, and Conneaut, Ohio. Again they found the labor punishing, but the strongest among them could manage a good day's wage while his stamina lasted. A newspaper in Conneaut calculated in 1899 that a shoveler, paid ten and one-half cents per ton, had to shovel nearly fifty tons (6,250 shovels-full, each weighing twenty pounds) to earn a five-dollar daily wage. But the major disadvantage of working on the docks was its seasonal nature, which put the men out of work through the long winter months. This practically guaranteed that they would spend their "off" months working in another seasonal industry, which had its peak activity during wintertime. So the Finns went off to the lumber camps for the winter — another low-paid, bone-wearying job to be sure, but one familiar to the Finnish immigrant.

LOGGING IN THE NORTHWOODS

Although the Finns arrived in Wisconsin at the end of the logging boom, they immediately became an integral part of the waning industry. Many had worked as loggers in their native land and were used to the physical hardships to be endured. They had an understanding for trees — how to notch and drop one into a small clearing without snagging the crown on other trees.

In the logging camps in which they were sheltered, the bunkhouse was usually a low-slung affair built of logs, with living quarters on one end and a cook shanty on the other, separated by an open breezeway. These were hastily built structures, meant for temporary shelter only as long as the trees in the immediate area might last, at which time the camp would be abandoned and the operations moved elsewhere. Thus many of the camps took on the appearance of a magpie's nest, lacking wooden floors and having perhaps a single door, one small window, and a tiny vent hole in the roof. The men slept in rough lumber bunks built along the walls around the large wood-burning stove. Straw served as a mattress, which soon became infested with lice. The "deacon's seat," a bench extending from the bottom tier of bunks, provided a place for the lumberjacks to sit in the evening, reading newspapers and magazines, mending clothes, whittling, and telling tall tales. The living quarters reeked of tobacco smoke, sweating bodies, and wet woolen socks, well-mingled with acrid, piney smoke from the heating stove.

The logging camp began to come to life each morning at about 3:30, when the cook and his assistant kindled fires in the kitchen and bunkhouse and began preparing breakfast for sixty to one hundred men.

Finska Ångfartygs Aktiebolaget, 1884–1908

The Finnish Steamship Company's Emigrant Hotel, in Hanko, near Helsinki, Finland. Many emigrants stayed here while waiting for their ships to depart Finland.

Finska Ångfartygs Aktiebolaget, 1884–1908

The Finnish Steamship Company's *Urania*, ca. 1893. This is the ship that brought Kristiina Niemistö to Hull, England, on the first leg of her journey to the United States in 1896.

WHi Image ID 53487

Early iron mine, Florence, Wisconsin, ca. 1880. Note shaft and windlass, ore bucket, and hand tools, lower right.

WHi Image ID 53485

Miners awaiting descent into an iron mine in Florence, Wisconsin. This mine is an example of later capital-intensive mining activity.

WHi Image ID 53603

The John Nieminen blacksmith and wagon shop, ca. 1912. Nieminen operated a shop near Withee, Wisconsin, from 1913 to 1945.

WHi Image ID 53600

Finns hauling hemlock bark for the tanning trade, near Brantwood, Wisconsin, in Price County

WHi Image ID 53491

Logging crew about to take to the woods near Humbird, Clark County, Wisconsin, ca. 1905

WHi Image ID 1960

Dinner time in the pinery, northern Wisconsin, ca. 1910

WHi Image ID 53490

Ole Emerson's crew skidding pine logs near Cable in Bayfield County, Wisconsin, during the winter of 1904

WHi Image ID 1958

Top loading a bobsled with part of the winter's harvest, ca. 1900

WHi Image ID 10565

WHi Image ID 53602

WHi Image ID 53493

Top: Agriculture in the cutover meant years of hard work pulling stumps from the fields. The farm shown is from Taylor County, Wisconsin, ca. 1895. *Middle:* Finnish family making hay near Brantwood, Wisconsin, in Price County. *Bottom:* A Finnish farmstead in the Midwestern cutover, ca. 1910.

At 4:00 a.m. the teamsters arose and harnessed and fed the horses in the barns. The lumberjacks rolled out of their bunks at 4:30, and in ten minutes sat down to a table of fried pork, potatoes, flapjacks, bread, and coffee. Then it was out into the woods to await sunup and the day's cutting. Many of the logging companies fed their workers out in the woods at noontime, and the men did not return to the bunkhouse until after dark.

In the woods there was a remarkable specialization of labor, with each man responsible for specific duties. Each camp had a foreman to keep order, and a cook with his assistants, or "flunkies," to prepare the meals. Choppers felled the trees with ax and crosscut saw, while sawyers "bucked" the logs into standard lengths of eight, ten, twelve, fourteen, and sixteen feet. Skidders dragged the logs with oxen or teams of horses from the stump to the loading areas, while swampers maintained the skid roads by cutting brush and in some camps by watering the icy skidways to reduce friction or drag. A top-loader stacked mammoth loads of logs on bobsleds, which were hauled away by teamsters who fed, drove, and cared for the draft animals. Large camps might also employ a blacksmith, carpenter, saw filer, and tally clerk as well.

Finns also went to the woods for forest products other than saw logs. They peeled hemlock bark and sold it to tanneries at Prentice and Tomahawk, which extracted the tannic acid for processing hides. Hemlock trees had to be peeled in May and June, but could not be hauled out of the swampy woods until late fall, after the ground had frozen and was covered with snow. Finns also cut cedar shingle bolts, riving and shaving them by hand into long wooden shingles called shakes. A good shingle-maker could shape two thousand shakes a day, and a few were able to make as many as three thousand.

Still another enterprise was hewing railroad ties with a broadaxe. These Finnish woodcutters preferred temperatures of minus-twenty degrees Fahrenheit, since then the frozen blocks of wood split easily along smooth planes. Other workers loaded the ties aboard railroad boxcars. They tipped each 380-pound tie up on one end, grasped it halfway down, and straightened up, tilting and balancing the load on one shoulder. Taking a running start, they ran up a sixteen-foot plank into the boxcar with the railroad tie, where it was stacked neatly in a row with others. These men were paid three cents per tie for loading, and often worked all night long by moonlight to finish before the morning freight train came along to pick up the boxcar.

Pulpwood cutting also figured largely in the local economy, though this work was usually done by farmers to supplement their wintertime income rather than by logging crews. All of the aforementioned occupations — mining, railroading, sailing, fishing, logging, factory and dockside work — proved popular with the Finn, but none was what he really sought. His days spent plowing and reaping in the Old Country beckoned in his memory, and he yearned for the good country life in his new home. It was the old dream once again: "Oma tupa, oma lupa." The Finns set about realizing this goal as soon as they were able.

CULTIVATING THE CUTOVER

It proved unfortunate for the Finns that their migration to Wisconsin occurred late in the nineteenth century. Immigrant pioneers had been settling in the state for almost half a century before the Finns began to arrive, and of course the best land was the first taken. Finns therefore had little to choose from except lands in those far-northern counties known as the "cutover." These were the old logging counties, now offered to the immigrants by railroads, logging companies, and real estate agents. Native-born Americans avoided the cutover, knowing the tremendous problems that it presented, but it was commonly said that foreign-born settlers were willing to work longer and harder while maintaining a lower standard of living than American settlers. Land salesmen seized upon the opportunity to unload this practically worthless cutover land on unsuspecting immigrants with dazzling newspaper advertisements.

Land agents also appealed to the Finn's cultural heritage, by drawing a parallel between land ownership and independence. The realtors not only suggested that a cutover farm would sustain a family in an economic sense, but that it would also raise the immigrant to a new social level within American society. A land promoter advertised in a Finnish American newspaper: "Take hold, Finland man, of the earth's surface, from which you made a living in Finland. Be your own master and boss! Let the inferior bow to the lords and listen to the blasts of the whistle." In 1917 land agent John A. Pelto placed newspaper advertisements describing the advantages of settling near Owen, Wisconsin, on "the best clayey soil in the state." The area boasted five railroad connections, eighteen cheese factories, several creameries, a pickle factory, and lumber mills that would buy the farmers' forest products as well as provide seasonal employment. All this at "terms so favorable that even the poorest could get started." In 1909 the G. F. Sanborn Company of Chicago promised to build a cabin sixteen-by-twenty-two feet for every purchaser of eighty acres of its holdings near Eagle River.

A bright future was painted by the land agents, but it was a vision not to be realized. "The best clayey soil in the state" was difficult to work and produced relatively low yields. The "free cabins" turned out to be rough board shacks covered with tarpaper. Roads, when they existed at all, were mere dirt ruts through the wilderness, which became bottomless quagmires in wet weather. Because of the lack of usable roads, many families arrived at their new home on the local freight train. After the engineer stopped the train as close as possible, the family climbed down, shouldered all of their possessions, and walked often a mile or more through the forest to find their stumpland farm. The John Niemistö family hired a teamster to take them to their new farm near Washburn, Bayfield County, in 1903. A mile from their destination the wagon trail ended, the goods were unloaded, and the freighter returned home. Mrs. Niemistö later recalled: "From among the goods I dug out a child's small cart. In it I placed a coffee pot, coffee, sugar, and milk. Our eldest daughter, who was five years of age, was told to push this extremely valuable load. A pack-sack of bread was placed on the shoulders of the four-year-old boy. My husband and I each took a child into our arms with as much more as we could carry. Then we started to track through the woods to a tar-paper shack that was waiting for its inhabitants."

Of course these primitive conditions improved over time, as more and more hopeful farmers moved into an area. But in spite of their hard work, the Finns were never able to control the one essential ingredient in their formula for success: the fertility of the soil upon which they settled.

The cutover lands of northern Wisconsin proved to be unsuitable for modern agriculture. The soil was generally unproductive, ranging from heavy red clay to light sand, and was usually low in humus, the organic matter necessary to high-yield agricultural crops in the days before chemical fertilizers. Vast areas were littered with boulders dropped by the glaciers thousands of years ago. The growing season was at best short, and a late thaw that delayed spring plowing or an early killing frost could wipe out an entire year's labor. The logged-over areas were covered with second-growth saplings and brush, and huge tree stumps left by the loggers remained firmly rooted in the "cleared" land. An enormous amount of labor would be necessary in settling a farm here, but the Finns were willing workers, and they were determined to return to the land as farmers.

Once the Finnish settler purchased a tract of cutover farmland, the entire family joined in the effort of preparing it for cultivation. The parents cut second-growth trees and chopped brush, piling it into heaps for wintertime burning. They blasted stumps out of the ground, or pulled them out with chains and horses, chopping through the roots as the massive tree stumps rolled over on their sides. Children grubbed the heavy clay off the roots, after which the stumps were burned or piled along the edges of fields to form fences. Fieldstones were also picked off the cropland to build dry walls and fences. It was possible to clear only two or three acres of land per year by hand, and a family's own labor was its only asset during these trying years. Families went through a difficult transitional period during settlement, when the husband shared the farmwork during the summer months, and then went back to the woods as a logger during the winter to provide a cash income. The wife and children remained on the farm year round, feeding and milking the cows, cleaning the barn and stable, clearing land, burning brush, cutting firewood, making fences, and in general readying the farm for full-time cultivation.

BUILDING A HOME

Ordinarily the family spent the first year on their farms living in a temporary shack or with neighbors until a permanent house could be built. The Finns built their farm buildings of hewn logs in the Scandinavian manner, so these structures look much different than Germanic log buildings found in southern Wisconsin. Generally the Scandinavians built all exterior walls of logs, carrying them right up to the gable peak; Germanic settlers ordinarily stopped building upward with logs at the eaves, and closed the gable peak with vertical board and batten siding. The Scandinavians shaped their logs for a better fit, while Germans tended to hew only the inner and outer surfaces, leaving tops and bottoms to follow their natural contour, sometimes with the tree bark left intact.

Finns used a home-made tool called a vara-rauta (scribe-iron) to aid in shaping logs. A roughly-hewn log was lifted into place on the topmost wall log, and one end of the long, V-shaped vara iron was run along the top of the lower log, as the other sharply pointed end cut or scribed a line in the upper timber exactly parallel to the lower. The top log was then removed, the axeman cut to the scribed line, and the log was replaced to check the fit. The trimming process might be repeated several times, until the top log fit tightly to the lower, this tight fit making chinking the house easier and more weather-tight than the loosely fitted German structure.

Germans hammered triangular-shaped blocks of wood between their wall logs, and plastered lime mortar over this rough-hewn lath to seal the spaces between the logs from the weather. The Finns, on the other hand, rounded the top surface of their logs to shed any water that might be driven in by the wind, and also hollowed the bottom surface to fit over the one below in a second-dimensional fit. A channel cut along the very center of the log's top was packed evenly with a layer of moss, and the upper log dropped over it to seal this organic chinking matter in place. The Finns also made frequent use of wooden pins to keep wall logs from sliding out of place; two-inch holes were bored through each pair of logs, and a large wooden pin was driven in place to lock them together. Even though frost might buckle or warp a wall, the logs were pinned together so tightly that none could fall out of place.

Largely because of available sources of supply, but also reflecting their ethnic traditions, Finns preferred to build of coniferous trees, especially white pine; Germans seemed to prefer oak logs even when pine was available. Some ethnic differences are also noted in the choice of roofing materials: both groups made use of hand-rived wooden shakes, sawed wooden shingles, and thatched roofs of rye straw. But the Finns also made use of other forest materials traditionally used in Norway, Sweden, and Finland. Some made roofs of vertically laid half-logs, hollowing the centers to form a trough and staggering the logs so that they alternated trough-peak-trough-peak across the roof. Another similar technique made use of vertical planks, a second layer nailed over the cracks separating the boards of the first layer. Birchbark was used in two different ways. In one, peeled birchbark was laid flat across closely-laid pole rafters, with a second layer of poles atop the bark to hold it in place. A variation was in turn to cover the layer of birchbark with four to six inches of prairie sod; a plank fastened at the eaves kept the earth in place, and a network of living roots laced the sod roof together against a storm.

In the Lake Superior region, almost none of the Finnish farmsteads bore more than a faint resemblance to the traditional enclosed farm building arrangement found in Finland, in which all structures opened into one or two central courtyards. In Wisconsin there was no traditional need to protect the farm against attacking soldiers or robbers as there had been in Finland. Landholdings here were also much larger than in the Old Country, so there was less need to crowd buildings together to conserve valuable cropland. Crowding would also increase the hazard of fire, since a fire in any one structure might destroy the entire farm. In Wisconsin one building might burn, but the others would remain relatively safe if sufficient space was left between.

But in some ways, the Wisconsin Finns did hold to traditional ideas of farm construction. They tended to build many small structures, each for its own particular function, rather than to build a few large multi-purpose buildings. This is another Scandinavian farming trait, in which small, isolated, largely self-sufficient farm units might consist of twelve, fourteen, sixteen, or more buildings. In addition to being traditional, this approach was also well suited to the Wisconsin Finn's pioneering existence. A farmer could more easily add a small log building to his farm as his own time permitted, rather than purchase sawed lumber and hire a crew to build a large structure. He could handle the short logs of modest-sized structures by himself or with perhaps one other helper, further freeing himself from the necessity of hiring workers. And besides, the cutover farm was slow to develop and large barns for storage purposes were not immediately necessary. The initial construction of a large full-blown farmstead was unwise if not economically impossible, and farms therefore evolved gradually over time.

The tupa, or dwelling, was usually the first structure to be built. The early ones were small, one-story, single-room log houses with hand-shaved shake roofs and rough-sawed lumber floors. This basic structure was later enlarged by adding log or frame sections as the family grew and prospered, or it was entirely replaced with a new, larger home. Furniture was homemade and simple: a table and benches, a "pie safe" cupboard for food storage, a rope- or slat-bed, perhaps a dry sink, and the ubiquitous wood-burning cook stove. Open wall shelves might contain a treasured clock or a few books, while coats and caps were hung on pegs driven into holes bored in the solid log walls. A wooden churn, spinning wheel, and baby cradle were among the first signs of domestic life, and a two-harness rug loom would soon follow.

A sauna, or bathhouse, was built immediately after the dwelling, and in some cases was even built first to serve as temporary quarters. The sauna was usually built from nine to twelve feet square, and was preferably located near a stream or lake. The logs were especially well-fitted, and the sauna often included an interior ceiling of poles covered with birchbark, which was in turn covered with six inches of earth for maximum heat retention. The earliest type of sauna to be built here in Wisconsin, called a "smoke sauna," was built without windows, having but a single small vent hole near the ceiling to allow smoke to escape from the chimneyless room. In one corner was built the heating stove of fieldstone, about four feet square and three feet high; the other walls were lined with wooden benches made of poplar, which absorbs less heat and therefore remains cooler to the touch than other types of lumber. The family began to fire the stove about two hours prior to bathing time, and watched the progress until the stones were heated to the desired temperature and the fire had burned down to coals. Someone then entered the smoke-filled room, leaving the door ajar and opening the vent hole, and tossed a dipperful of water on the hot stones. The resultant gush of steam carried the smoke along outside through the vent, the door and vent were closed, the benches wiped clean of soot, and the bathing began.

Most Finns took a "dry sweat" first, just sitting naked in the hot room until the body began to sweat. Then they threw water on the hot stones to produce steam, temperatures sometimes rising to 150 degrees Fahrenheit. The bathers periodically ran outdoors to plunge into the nearby lake, stream, or snowbank, and they whipped each other's skin with a vihta, or switch of cedar or birch boughs, to stimulate blood circulation. Later saunas were "civilized" by adding a dressing room to the steam room so that bathers were not forced to run naked from house to sauna in winter, and they were further improved by substituting an iron box stove for the fieldstone oven. The iron stove was covered with a layer of stones to absorb heat, and a chimney carried the smoke away.

The sauna was used for purposes other than bathing. Occasionally it was used to smoke meat or to dry various natural products used in the farm's economy, such as willow bark for tanning hides. The sauna was preferred by midwives for childbirth, both because it was heated and therefore was relatively sterile, and also because its warmth aided the expectant mother's muscles in relaxing. It was often used to break up an on-coming cold or headache, reflecting the Finn's preference for health via vigorous exercise and proper diet rather than through the use of patent medicines or pills. According to a Finnish proverb, "If sauna and brandy cannot help a man, death is near at hand."

The next structure to be built was probably the navetta, or cowbarn, as a cow or two was needed to furnish the family's milk and butter. These were small, primitive affairs, later replaced with larger dairy barns as the farm's economy shifted from self-sufficient to commercial dairying. The Finns in Wisconsin continued their Old World specialization of labor, in which the men did the bulk of the field work to raise feed crops, and the women tended the cattle. The women usually cleaned the barn, fed the livestock, and milked the cows, as these chores were considered woman's work amongst the Finns; many men did not know how to milk a cow until their farms warranted a milking machine in later years.

Two crops predominated for use as animal fodder: timothy hay and rutabagas. Timothy hay was the real pioneer crop, as it could withstand poor soil, marshy conditions, and total neglect. During the early years of settlement it could be planted amongst stumps and stones in the roughly cleared fields, since the entire crop was harvested by hand. The Finns built a lato, or haybarn, right in a hayfield, and this structure might serve several adjacent fields. The hay was cut with a scythe, raked together by hand, and carried and hand-pitched into the diminutive storage barns. As in Finland, a small cart-load at a time would then be carried to the farmyard to feed the stock. This lessened the need for a team of horses (if the farmer pulled the cart) and also lessened the danger of fire by leaving the combustible hay some distance from the farm buildings. After the farmer had purchased a team of horses and cleared the hayfields of stumps and stones, he cut his hay crop with a mower, raked and loaded it onto wagons with horsepower, and filled the barns with the aid of a mechanical harpoon fork and haytrack mounted under the barn's ridge.

Since corn would not grow to maturity in northern Wisconsin's short growing season, rutabagas were raised for cowfeed as a substitute for the corn ensilage fed to cattle in the southern parts of the state as moist win-tertime feed. Children were given the tedious job of hand-planting the black, pinhead-sized rutabaga seeds in long rows. Later they thinned the rows on hands and knees, and during the summer hoed weeds. At harvest time the melon-sized roots were pulled up by hand, tops and secondary roots slashed off, and the "bagas" tossed into a waiting wagon for transport to the farmyard. Once in the yard they were unloaded into storage bins, often built as root cellars underground to keep the feed safe from frost. They were chopped or sliced before being fed to livestock.

The last major farm structure, a talli, or horse stable, was built a few years after the cowbarn. Many families could not afford to purchase horses upon arrival, and were obliged to hire teams for heavy labor such as plowing or skidding logs. As soon as a team could be purchased, a small stable was built to shelter the valuable draft animals, and wild hay, timothy hay, and oats were fed to them. Oats were the most popular of the cereal crops among the Finns, in part because the plant was hardy and would thrive even in northern Wisconsin, and also because the livestock could eat the entire plant — kernels, straw, and all.

Wisconsin Finns also built grain-related structures, although these buildings were relatively few in number since farmers almost immediately turned to dairying rather than to cash-crop grain farming. One finds an occasional aitta, or granary, on Finnish farms, though they were primarily used to store oats for animal feed rather than wheat or rye for human consumption or cash sale as they would have been in Finland. Instead, in Wisconsin, they existed as isolated units, at most one per farm, and not in rows as they commonly do in Finland. The riihi, or threshing barn, is even more scarce, because of the introduction of the threshing machine among American farmers prior to the Finns' arrival. The riihi was used both to dry and thresh grain; some had lean-to additions for straw storage as well. A chimneyless fieldstone or brick oven was located in one corner of the main room, sauna fashion, which generated heat to dry the grain. Sheaves were placed on a series of loosely spaced poles that formed an interior ceiling, and the oven was fired to drive off moisture. When sufficiently dry, the sheaves were taken down and threshed out a few at a time with a flail on the riihi floor, a laborious procedure rendered obsolete by the threshing machine. In addition, Wisconsin farmers were not plagued with a late-summer rainy season as in Finland, so crops could dry more thoroughly outdoors without providing an extra building for this purpose.

One Finnish-built structure deserves special mention as a unique example of Old World culture: the Davidson windmill, located east of Superior on State Highway 13, on a high bluff overlooking the Amnicon River valley. This flour mill was built by Jaako Tapola, who had been a millwright in his native Finland until he immigrated to America and settled on the Amnicon River in 1887. Tapola later anglicized his name to Jacob Davidson, a practice common among the Finns, whose names were often mispronounced by their new American neighbors. Davidson built the mill of local materials around 1900, his only help being his children. The eight-sided log tower is topped with a revolving turret that turns on wooden rollers, so that the sails could be swung into and out of the wind. Eight wooden arms, or wings, were covered with canvas sailcloth to catch the Lake Superior winds while grinding flour; the sails were furled during slack periods. Davidson himself fashioned the hardwood gearing and shafts, and also cut the millstones from rock found in the Amnicon river bed. The mill was able to grind about forty barrels of flour per day, and often the grinding continued all night long to take advantage of good winds. The mill stands empty today, a reminder of a lifestyle long since vanished from the landscape.

CONGREGATIONS AND COMMUNITIES

Finnish social institutions have perhaps proved more durable than their architectural remnants. As soon as they arrived in America, the Finns sought each other's companionship, maintaining old ties rather than allowing them to vanish in the mainstream of American society. As newcomers to a strange land, they attempted to establish a familiar social order, drawing upon their cultural heritage to found a rich variety of associative organizations. Their world became crowded with churches, temperance societies, workingmen's associations, newspapers, co-operatives, and other institutions. "Everyone is setting up something," commented an Old Country bishop, "even the children, leaving only the cat at home." Finnish immigrants were primarily Protestant and Lutheran. In 1900 more than ninety-eight percent of the entire population of Finland was listed as communicants of the state-supported church, with only a scattering of Greek and Roman Catholics, Methodists, and others. The immigrant churches naturally reflected this heritage. In 1936 there were twenty-five Finnish congregations, all Lutheran, in Wisconsin settlements such as Superior, Iron Belt, Owen, Phelps, Westboro, Maple, North York, Clifford, and Washburn. Reflecting an old and widespread schism, the congregations were grouped into three distinct religious bodies: the

Finnish Apostolic Lutheran Church, the Finnish National Lutheran Church, and the Suomi Synod. The first of these stemmed from the influential Lars Levi Laestadius religious awakening of the early nineteenth century in northern Finland and Sweden. In 1936 there were eight Apostolic congregations in Wisconsin, of which seven were rural with a membership of 911. The second group, the Finnish National Church, organized in 1898 in Rock Springs, Wyoming, had in the same year nine parishes in Wisconsin, of which eight were rural, with a total membership of 446. The third, the Suomi Synod, the American transplant of the Finnish state church, founded in Calumet, Michigan, in 1890, became the strongest of the Finnish religious bodies in America, counting eight congregations in Wisconsin, seven of which were rural, with 566 members in 1936. The Finnish congregations tended to be small and rural in character, and their church buildings were humble and unpretentious.

Many temperance societies were likewise launched by the immigrants. The first of these institutions appeared in 1890 in West Superior and Montreal in Iron County. By 1910 similar groups, bearing picturesque and appropriate titles (Hope of Our Fathers, Life, Light, Hero), had arisen in seven other settlements as well, including Hurley, Iron Belt, Maple, Van Buskirk, Redgranite, Turtle Lake, and Waino. Their combined membership probably ranged from 350 to 500. These institutions were much more than crusaders against the evils of intemperance. Many of them assumed significant fraternal, cultural, and social functions. They provided illness and funeral benefits, sponsored dramatic and choral groups, bands, and debating clubs. They also established libraries and reading rooms containing well-thumbed books and newspapers from the Old Country, and endeavored to cater to the recreational needs of the immigrants through folk games and dancing festivals. Many of the Wisconsin societies were short-lived, however, and not many witnessed the rise and fall of the Prohibition Amendment.

After the turn of the century, new institutional enterprises emerged on the horizon to compete with the church and the temperance society. Workers' associations began to attract the support of many immigrants. Initially they took on the character of Imatra societies, being essentially idealistic, nonrevolutionary, and nonpolitical. However, with the organization of the Finnish Socialist Federation in Hibbing, Minnesota, in 1906, they were for the most part quickly transformed into socialist locals. In that year there were three fairly strong locals in the state, at Kenosha, Milwaukee, and Superior, with a combined membership of seventy. By 1917 the number had increased to ten societies having a total membership of 336, located at Allouez, Iron Belt, Maple, Racine, Oulu, Brantwood, and Clifford. The Finnish socialist movement, as well as the American organizations with which it was integrated, felt the impact of schismatic forces such as the 1914 IWW revolt headed by Leo Laukki, and the communist uprising of 1919–1920. While several of these workers' groups still survive, especially in Superior, their history, as well as that of societies long since disbanded, seems to suggest that they have been more successful as cultural and social agencies than as advocates of class struggle. They will most likely be remembered for the excellent dramatic societies, speakers' organizations, musical groups, and athletic teams that have appeared under their aegis.

Journalism, too, has found an important place in the institutional life of the Wisconsin Finns. Several influential Finnish-language newspapers have been printed in Superior and elsewhere. Among those that appeared in the state but are now either dead or have been transferred to other states are the *Lapatossu* and the *Punikki*, popular humor sheets with a pronounced socialist bias; the feminist *Työläisnainen*; the *Siirtolainen*, which, after having been moved East, was returned to Duluth, Minnesota, where it expired in 1937; and a farm journal, the *Pelto ja Koti*. One long-lived newspaper was published in Superior from 1914 through 1998, the *Työmies*, a working-class organ generally sympathetic with the communist cause.

It has been, perhaps, in the field of the consumers' co-operative movement that the Finnish immigrants of Wisconsin have fashioned their most enduring monument. A co-operative is a business voluntarily owned and controlled by its member patrons, and operated by them on a non-profit or cost basis. Group members pool their purchasing power, order large shipments of goods, and then distribute these goods among the members at cost. Some co-operatives might hire a manager, who handles the ordering, stocks the shelves, and conducts the daily business as an agent of the membership. Any "profits" or surplus funds are returned to the members at the end of the operating year after all bills are paid by the organization. Finnish co-operators from Iron River, Wisconsin, and Hancock, Michigan, initiated the steps leading to the establishment of the Central Cooperative Wholesale at Superior in 1917. The enlarged organization which had outlets in Wisconsin, Michigan, and Minnesota increased its annual sales from $25,574 in 1917 to nearly $5,000,000 in 1941. In this latter year 126 local societies were affiliated with the CCW, twenty-nine of them located in Wisconsin. While not all of these co-ops were sponsored by Finns, the drive as well as the leadership came from the Finnish group.

Since the end of World War II, Finnish co-operatives have been undergoing changes. In the first place, reliance on the Finnish language has been dropped and a more Americanized institution has evolved. The political fervor of the early co-operative movement has also mellowed. The rise of chain stores and supermarkets pushed many of the small co-ops into financial ruin, but even today co-ops can be found in the Finnish settlement areas of the state.

THE TRADITIONAL LIFE

In addition to the Finns' associative spirit, they maintained various other cultural traits brought along from their homeland. They celebrated Juhannus at midsummer, June 24, as well as Vappu, or May Day. These festive occasions were observed with rousing speeches, songs, poetry reading, outdoor drama, and various sporting events such as calisthenics, discus throwing, and foot races. Housewives began cooking soup in huge copper boilers during the early morning hours, which they later brought to the picnic and shared with all present. In the evening the celebrants often built smudge fires in stumps and brush piles to drive mosquitoes away from the festivities.

Their domestic life in some ways closely resembled life in Finland, especially among first-generation immigrants. A Finn might jump across the doorsill upon entering the home at night, so that the Kaahura (spook) could not get hold of the heel left behind the other. They resorted to the ancient practice of bleeding to purge the body of impurities. A kuppisarvi, or horn cup, was fashioned from the shaved tip of a cowhorn, and a bit of calf bladder was tied over the small end. The afflicted part of the body was then cut or lanced to begin the bleeding process. The large, open end of the horn was placed over the wound, and suction was applied by drawing on the small end of the horn with the mouth. The blood flowed into the partial vacuum created inside the horn, and the membrane allowed air to pass out of the horn without eliminating the vacuum. The patient usually retired to the sauna after bleeding, and then to bed for a good night's rest.

Finns created all manner of handmade items during early settlement. Many of them kept a few sheep to provide wool, which they washed, carded, spun, and either wove or knitted into warm woolen underwear, socks, mittens, and sweaters. They wove narrow belts on hand-carved heddle looms, and made their own shoes, called shoepacks, of home-tanned cowhide. They made their footwear with slightly upturned, pointed toes because they all but lived on skis in the wintertime and did not want to strap their feet too tightly to the ski bindings. Finns wanted their feet to be free to slip out of the ski strap in case of a bad fall, thus preventing broken bones and twisted limbs. They carved their own skis, fashioned snowshoes, and whittled fish-net bobbins, fishing floats, fish-line reels, and hook boxes. They also made knives out of old files, attaching bone or antler handles to the steel blades.

The Finns settling in rural Wisconsin maintained a pioneer existence far later than most immigrant groups, building their homes and farms in the traditional styles by traditional methods long after other immigrants had made the transition to American balloon-framed architecture. They made their own shoes and wove their own cloth when other groups had abandoned their folkways in favor of American factory-made goods. Part of this was due to the Finns' poverty upon arrival: they made their own shoes because they could not afford to pay cash for them, and a farmer's own labor was in a sense "free." Part of their apparent fondness for traditional ways might also reflect their late arrival: after all, they came to Wisconsin some sixty years after the beginning of the influx of groups such as the Germans and Norwegians, who had been assimilating into American society for over two generations when the Finns began to arrive. A third often-cited reason, but one which defies scientific examination, is that the Finns were traditional by nature: they were primarily rural peasants recently removed from a traditional culture, and were slower to adopt new ways than urban immigrants from industrial societies. But perhaps most importantly, the Finns tended to settle together and created little Finlands wherever they went. This cultural reinforcement allowed them to live independently of "foreign" or non-Finnish language and ways; their own language, both written and oral, their associative spirit, their desire to maintain familiar ways under new freedoms found in the United States, permitted the Finns to exist as an independent ethnic community well into the twentieth century.

WHi Image ID 53601

This house shows Scandanavian construction techniques with closely fitted logs that did not need the addition of plaster to seal the spaces between the logs. Henry Getto house at Oulu, Wisconsin, in Bayfield County, ca. 1945.

WHi Image ID 3988

The Christian Turck house in the village of Germantown, Wisconsin, Washington County, ca. 1910. The Germanic tradition of house construction used loosely-fitted logs and a rough lath as a base for a lime-mortar plaster that was used to seal the spaces between the logs.

WHi Image ID 53441

A typical pioneer Finnish sauna, ca. 1947, near Brantwood, Wisconsin. Saunas were often the first building constructed on a newly settled farm.

WHi Image ID 53964

The original dwelling of the Niemistö's. A typical Finnish log cabin, rough but eminently satisfactory in the pioneering era, ca. 1947, near Washburn, Wisconsin.

WHi Image ID 53599

The Jacob Davidson (Jaako Tapola) windmill, near Superior, Wisconsin. The mill was built ca. 1900. Davidson hand carved the huge wooden gears that turned the millstone.

WHi Image ID 4476

The Wentworth Farmers' Cooperative in Wentworth, Wisconsin, ca. 1947. The coop was organized in 1919 by a group of Finnish, Norwegian, and Swedish farmers.

WHi Image ID 4479

The Cooperative Marketing Store in Maple, Wisconsin, served as a gathering place for local shoppers.

WHi Image ID 53442

The Tarmo Boarding House on Third Street in Superior, Wisconsin, was established in 1912. It was run cooperatively with most of the members tending to be single men. Rooms were provided and meals of traditional Finnish food were served.

WHi Image ID 53444

Finnish Workers' Hall, ca. August 1947, in Superior, Wisconsin

WHi Image ID 53445

This rural Suomi Synod Church was built in Waino, Wisconsin, around 1900. Services at the church were abandoned in 1968 and it was renamed Waino Pioneer Chapel.

WHi Image ID 53446

The Little Finland Cabins was a popular tourist camp on highway US-2 in Hurley, Wisconsin, near the border with Michigan's upper peninsula. The camp was built by the Saari brothers around 1936. The camp featured an American version of the traditional Finnish sauna.

Konsta Sorvisto cards wool to prepare for spinning as his wife, Johanna, makes yarn with her spinning wheel near Oulu, Wisconsin, in Bayfield County.

WHi Image ID 53597

The local Finnish community gathers at the Henry Cass Kasurinen farm, near Withee, Wisconsin, for a play presented outdoors.

The Työmies Publishing Company building in Superior, Wisconsin. The *Työmies* newspaper was published in Superior from 1914 until 1998. Although chiefly a socialist newspaper, its contacts with the Finnish labor societies allowed the newspaper to report and photograph local cultural news including plays, musicals, and other events sponsored by the local labor halls.

FROM KÖYHÄJOKI KAUSTINEN TO FLORIDA

by Kristiina Niemistö
translated from the original Finnish by Maija Salo Cravens

The following account was written by Kristiina Niemistö, who emigrated to America from Köyhäjoki near Kaustinen in western Finland. She was a young, single girl when she traveled here in 1896. This account was written and published at a later point in her life, after she and her family had moved from Wisconsin to Florida. Kristiina's story was originally serialized in the Finnish language newspaper, Auttaja *(The Helper), in Ironwood, Michigan, between November 1944 and February 1945. Although she feels that "most of the events would be mundane to my readers for the majority of them [Finnish immigrants] have traveled the same road," her richly detailed story describes her hardships and experiences in traveling to a new country and her resourcefulness and strength in adapting to a new culture. This account is reprinted with permission of the Lutheran Church-Missouri Synod.*

There's many a twist and turn in the path of life.... There are also many pitfalls and traps in the road of life. But God watches over us.

In the year 1896, March 27, I left my home for the wide world.

Just like yesterday, I remember the moment when I closed the beloved door of my childhood home. With a heavy heart I bid goodbye to my loved ones, to many for the last time. Mother's words stayed in my mind forever, "Have faith in God, take Jesus with you on your travels. He will safeguard you from the temptations you will meet in the world."

"Don't worry, Mother, I will take care of myself, I won't fall into temptation that easily!"

Father took the traveler as far as Kokkola. From there I continued on to Hankoniemi after a day's wait. At Hankoniemi, a ship called [*Urania*] was waiting for passengers. Soon everyone was told to get onboard, passports were checked, and then the ship took off. Then we cheered and waved our handkerchiefs.

Hankoniemi and Finland disappeared beyond the horizon. Goodbye, Finland, goodbye. The national anthem was sung with fresh, strong voices. Finland could not be seen anymore.

But it's hard to repress a young heart. When you have young blood in your veins, nothing frightens you. Even the waves were singing their joy.

In the evening, my mind got more somber, when there was no sign of a bed. My cousin said, "Don't look for a place to sleep, just put your bag under your head and go to sleep." To eat we had hard bread and to drink mild beer. Many days passed before we arrived in England.

It was nice to get onshore where seasickness didn't affect us anymore.

Onshore, drivers were waiting for us and took us around town. The horses pulling us were big. The town was beautiful and there were memorial statues in every street corner.

While we waited we went sightseeing for two days before an old ship called *Laurentia* set off for the Atlantic. The sea was calm and soon everyone went into their cabins. There we ate food brought from home, unpeeled potatoes and hard bread. And since I ate meals like this, I didn't get seasick.

There were also some uncomfortable moments on the ship. There was a man who spoke to me many times when we went on deck in the morning. I told my cousin that the next time the man comes near me I'd slap him. The next morning we went on deck again and the man approached me again. I had learned the English words "get out" and I uttered them while hitting him hard enough to send him sprawling on the deck. People around me cheered. I was afraid I would be punished for what I did but I never saw the man again.

Finally the long voyage was over. Early in the morning we arrived at the harbor of Halifax. Oh, how we sang and laughed when we saw land again! In the course of the day, we were allowed ashore. We thanked God for getting us across the ocean without greater difficulties.

Everyone else was taken to the customs hall but Liisa and I were taken alone into another room where an old man was sitting. I urged Liisa to leave with me. Liisa was afraid to leave, she thought we'd be punished for rejecting and hitting the gentleman on the ship. I observed the others getting on a train and I picked up my suitcase and ran after them. At first I was afraid that it might be the wrong train, but the conductor took our tickets and it just happened to be the right train. The train traveled the whole day. Finally the train stopped and we were told that we had to stay there for a while. Some people got off the train; Liisa and I stayed alone on the train. Soon two men entered. One was a Finn, with him there was an English man with a sheaf of papers in his hand. The Finn explained that the train would stay here overnight and that we could go into a free hotel for the night. I snapped at him that we would not move an inch but would stay on the bench the whole night. The men left in a hurry.

The next day we traveled through the heartland of Canada. After looking at the scenery for a while we opened the bunk above the bench and went to sleep. I hadn't been asleep for long when Liisa awoke me to look at the water over the tracks. I said I didn't care. I didn't get to sleep very long until we heard the sound of water surging and pounding. Then the car fell over and I fell out of bed. The door was stuck so we couldn't get out of the car. The last car had stayed upright and people from there came to our aid. Soon they were able to open the window, and we were lifted out of the car one by one.

What a terrifying sight we encountered when we got out of the car. The engine had left the tracks and taken many cars with it. Both legs of the conductor were stuck under the train and he died before help arrived. The bodies of two young boys leaned against a car. One's eye was hanging over his cheek and blood streamed out of his mouth. A fourteen-year-old boy went missing and his body was never found. I thank God that He didn't let us die without faith.

In that terrible, horror-filled place we had to wait for hours before help arrived. Finally the doctors, ambulances and photographers arrived. When they were done, we were finally allowed to leave the site of the accident, but the bleeding and screams of the injured and dying left a bad memory.

We were gathered in a herd like cattle and ordered to walk along the railroad. Near the site of the accident the railroad was in such bad shape that it wobbled under foot. After walking for a while we started to see freight cars in front of us. We continued our journey onboard those and naturally the ride was not very good. We were, however, grateful that somehow we got out of the heartland where the train had left the tracks.

After a while we arrived at a town. Somebody had set up tables at the crossroads where the travelers could get something to eat. When we had had something to eat and drink and rested a while, we again boarded a real passenger train on which we continued our journey to Montreal, Quebec. There a Finnish agent met us and we were well taken care of.

As soon as possible we bought tickets to Ironwood. This was finally the last leg of our journey. The trip went well and we didn't encounter any adversities. On April 28th, 1896 we arrived at the train station in Ironwood. We were met by uncle Joonas' son Heikki and uncle Jukka's

son Juhani. It was great fun to see them after the long time we had traveled in a strange country unable to speak the language. We went from the
station to the Pihlaja diner by street-car. And there we encountered a
room full of people from Kaustinen! There was Jooperi and Kalle Kause
and the brothers Penttilä and many other former inhabitants of our
home village. I let out a sigh of relief at being able to congregate among
familiar old friends. The feelings of dread and horror slowly dissipated.
The long and arduous journey was beginning to feel like a bad dream.

Having rested a bit, we started to look for work with Mrs. Kykyri. We
were warned that it would be a useless effort for there were many girls
without work. We were told that these unemployed girls went to the bread
line to eat and that there was no hope of work. It seemed like the road
was rising against us. I said to Liisa that it seemed our hopes had been in
vain. It really seemed like a black cloud was hovering over our dreams.

America seemed very dark. Looking around we noticed that even
some of the older inhabitants were unemployed; how could we newly arrived from the old country find work? The world really seemed hopeless.

But then totally unexpectedly life became light and hopeful again.
Mrs. Pihlaja came to talk to us when we were in a state of despair. She
had a joyful message for us. She said that a man called Matti Kuusisto
needed a maid for a month. The next day I went to work, at least for a
month. Things were looking good.

I had been in Ironwood for one month and three days when I received a letter from home in Finland. My joy at getting the letter turned
into sorrow upon reading it. My dear father had died. . . . It suddenly felt
unbearable. If only I had known! I would never have left home. It was
probably too much for him to bear, to let a child go so far away. It was
my fault that he died. . . .

These kinds of recriminations, insurmountable to me, arose from my
broken heart. I didn't know where to turn to. I had heard that there was
a pastor Kivi in Ironwood who was a good preacher. Towards his church
I directed my steps. I wanted to learn what kind of people get to heaven.
I had doubts about my father's state. Had he really gone to heaven? The
letter had assured that he had died in faith.

The text of the sermon was Matthew 27. The sermon made it clear
that the death and resurrection of Jesus was the base of everyone's sal-
vation. Even the temple curtain had split. Now every Christian has the
right to enter the holiest place through Jesus' blood.

This sermon stayed with me forever. I now believed that father had gone to heaven. I myself still had a lot of obstacles. I felt too young to abandon the company and fun of young people. I could think of a lot of reasons. So I finally decided to remember forever what Pastor Kivi had said and then at a suitable moment I would become a believer. So it was that I left it until later.

Soon after this came the biggest change in my life so far. I met my life companion.

I married John Niemistö on March 30th, 1897. Soon after the wedding he left for Colorado, a town called Telluride, where he had a brother, Emanuel Niemistö. I stayed in Ironwood until my husband acquainted himself with the new place and found work, etc. I didn't leave for Colorado until June.

On June 18th, early in the morning, the train left the station in Ironwood. By 8 o'clock we were already in Ashland. All I could think about was seeing my dear spouse again. The next day we were in Omaha where I had a two-hour wait for the train.

After spending a few moments inside the station, I went to stand outside. While leaning against the wall I fainted. I was taken (I found out afterwards) to the hospital, and the train of course left without me. I woke up in the hospital not knowing how long I had been lying there. Upon wakening and realizing that I was in a strange place, dread and fear came upon me. I didn't know what to do. My mind was totally confused. Next to me there was a woman with huge boils all over her body. I tried to indicate with what little English I had that I needed water to drink. Finally she rang a bell and a nurse arrived. I was terribly thirsty. When she finally arrived she only shook her head. I didn't get any water. There was a big clay pot on the table in the room. When the nurse left I went to look in the pot. I was so thirsty that I was determined to dip my tongue in whatever the vessel held. I didn't get any water all night. The pot was empty. The thirst just kept getting worse.

I had other things to worry about as well. Where were my clothes? Where was my ticket? Where had God led me? Will I ever see my husband again? Oh, what a terrible fate this is. My husband would never know what happened to me. I felt like even God wasn't looking after me, although I started thinking about Kivi's sermon again. Oh, why didn't I believe then? It must be too late by now! I had lost my ticket to heaven as well as my earthly ticket.

If only morning would come so I could see how things were. Finally the door to the room opened and the nurse arrived carrying a tray of food. To her question of how I was, I answered: well. I tried to act as if I was feeling well and I ate everything that was placed in front of me. Again I tried to talk about my ticket and clothes. The nurse talked a lot but I didn't understand what she said. At 9 o'clock, a doctor arrived. After examining me he indicated 10 on the clock and left. I didn't understand what he had said to me. That gave me another cause for worrying. What will happen to me at 10 o'clock? I endured a long, anxious hour. I couldn't even cry any more.

Although slowly, the hour finally passed. The doctor and two nurses came into my room. They opened a door in the corner and took out my clothes and dressed me. They kissed me, caressed my cheeks and started to comb my hair. That wasn't an easy task and finally they just braided my hair and that was that.

Again I started to talk about my ticket and the train. We went down a long staircase and out of the hospital. There stood a handsome two-seater carriage with a pair of handsome horses in front of it. One of the nurses sat down next to the driver, the other next to me and so we departed for the unknown. The road followed a shallow but beautiful riverbank for a long way.

But the journey was long and my mind somber because I had not found out where we were going. Finally it seemed like we had arrived. A big building stood in front of us and there we stopped. Where was I? Was this another hospital?

After gazing at it for a while, joy began to fill my heart. This was the very railway station where I had fainted. I then tried to make my companions understand that they had brought me here for nothing for I didn't have a ticket anymore. They just laughed and half lifted me out of the carriage and walked me to the station. And there we found all my belongings including my wallet and ticket. How good it felt!

Three wives had come into the station with some bags of fruit and some kind of gelatin that they mixed with water to drink. After a while I understood I wasn't supposed to drink plain water. Soon the train arrived and I was able to continue my journey. A bench for just me to sit on was found and then bidding me goodbye the nurses and the doctor left. I was left to sit by myself and think about the goodness of these strangers. I was forced to think about how I had neglected to do good works for others.

Water isn't expensive but if you give it to someone in the spirit of love, it is of God. My thoughts were interrupted by the sight of the Colorado mountains. Again my heart was struck by fear. On one side there were only tall, dark mountains, on the other a deep river valley. Will this be my grave? I thought that God had been pulling me towards Him because my death was near. But poor me, I had hardened my heart! The Lord warns not to harden your heart if you hear His voice. I thought about my child-hood in Finland, particularly the time of catechism school when I had found grace. How good it had felt then. Those days when I was in cate-chism school, Pastor Krohn was the parson at Kaustinen. After that time the enemy had won me back into the world. I wasn't sure anymore of having God's grace. Right now things were different for I was convinced that there was no grace for me anymore.

Through my meditation I heard the word "Denver" and knew that I still had one more day to travel. Excited I waited for the moment when they would call "Telluride." At 6 o'clock the train arrived at the station and my husband was there to meet me. For everyone who has experi-enced these feelings they are familiar. My joy was great at having finally arrived.

One thing I wondered about, namely the fact that there was still snow on the ground although it was Midsummer's Eve. My husband as-sured me that it would soon melt but in the same breath he told me that the snow on top of the mountains would never melt. The mines where the men worked were on top of the mountains. They lived there and came to town only once a month. I tended to get bored but after a while I bided my time cleaning people's houses and some such stuff.

Having lived there for two years, our first child was born. Our life was now happy! But we were not done with sorrow yet. The child was about five months old when I got seriously ill. Every day at about 4 in the afternoon, a fever would come upon me. Even the doctor thought I had no hope of ever getting well. After bothering me for a while the fever started to let go. But now a new danger arose for my body temperature got too low. The doctors didn't know what to do.

The doctor said that a low body temperature is much more danger-ous than the fever itself. I was given stimulants to keep up circulation. The child of course was taken away from me and that also slowed my recov-ery. Also the child became feverish.

These adversities seemed hard to endure and I started to question

what bad deeds I had done for God to test me so harshly. But then I realized that not believing is the greatest sin. The old me still fought against
this with all my might. I didn't have the strength to believe in Christ. But
in my mind these words went around that a human being can't get near
to God or believe in Him on his own powers or reason. In my heart I
pleaded for God to give me strength to believe and that nothing worse
would happen to me.

In the year 1900 my brother Matti came to America. First he went to
Scofield where my brother Antti lived. He found work immediately and
wrote to me that he was coming to visit us in Telluride.

It wasn't long after that I heard terrible news from Finland. There
had been an accident at the Scofield mine and hundreds of men had
died. There had been some kind of an explosion in the mine. Worried,
with a trembling heart, I perused the names of the dead in the newspapers. I was afraid that both my brothers had lost their lives in the accident. Having examined the list I was at first happy for I hadn't found the
name Jacobson at all. But then I noticed a familiar name, Peltokangas.
What if that was my brother Matti for he had used that name in Finland!

After a few days I received a letter which proved that my fears had
not been for nothing. The letter was from my brother Antti and in it he
wrote that brother Matti had indeed died in that accident as well as some
other more distant relatives.

The reader can well surmise what kind of thoughts filled my mind.
My old mother now came into my thoughts. How would she be able to
bear this message? Father is no longer there to give her comfort but she's
all alone with her grief. And Matti was only able to stay here for a little
more than a month before he died and I didn't even get to see him.

I thought that as soon as my husband gets home from work I would
suggest to him that we get out of this place. There wasn't even a pastor
here to comfort me in my grief. Only once did I get to hear a sermon in
the course of three and a half years when a Finnish missionary visited
the locale. And even he didn't really preach a sermon, just talked about
this and that.

When my husband came home the next time I talked to him about
moving. And so it was that we soon decided to leave Colorado. We directed our way towards Minnesota, to a town called Sparta. We arrived
there on Nov. 20, 1900. Right away I searched out the Finnish pastor of
the town. The pastor in those days was Pastor Havukainen but even his

sermons could not fulfill me. If I remember correctly, the late Pastor Rankila arrived in 1902. I went to hear the new preacher. I had heard that he was one of the followers of Hedberg. . . .

One night my husband went to visit the neighbors. Upon his return he said that tomorrow he, along with Matti Pakkala and Matti Heikkilä, would leave for Washburn, Wisc. to take a look at some land. He even brought pictures with him. They depicted handsome deer, big trout and fat sockers. All these you can take without permits, he explained. On the shores of Lake Superior there is a beautiful town with several churches. That was the paradise they had decided to go see.

According to the plan agreed upon the previous night, my husband left with two of our neighbors to Washburn, Wisc. to see about the land. The region looked promising so they each took 40 acres. It must have looked really good because when they returned home they declared that in a week we would leave to establish a home there.

We'd have to take all our belongings with us so the men went to order a railway car. The meager furniture of all three families was loaded into it. There was even a cow and there was no other choice but to push it into the car with the furniture. A guard was also needed so Matti Heikkilä decided to travel in the freight car to watch over the cow and the belongings.

We left for Washburn on April 21, 1904. With sadness we took leave of our relatives and friends once again and left for a home that didn't even exist yet. The next night was spent in Duluth. In the morning we left for Washburn. We were allowed to stay in the rooms of the land company. The building had a big second floor made up of a single room. A set of wobbly, creaky stairs led up there from the outside. That is where our three families lived for a while. Each family had small children who were so delighted by the wobbly stairs that they wanted go up and down the stairs repeatedly. That was so nerve-wracking that finally I told my husband to go and make a cabin on our own land even if he had to build it out of turf, for it was impossible to watch the children all the time to keep them from hurting themselves on the stairs.

Naturally we had no building materials. My husband went and bought a thousand feet of rough boards and two rolls of tar paper and made a cabin out of them. And it didn't even take many days. On the first day of June we moved into our new home.

Getting there, however, was no easy task. There was no road. A car-

riage road went part of the way but the rest we had to walk along a narrow path in the undergrowth. In the morning my husband hired some
horses. Our belongings were put on the cart, and the children and I were
put on top of the load. The family had grown to four children, the oldest of whom was five years old. Two of youngest ones couldn't walk yet.
Sitting with the children on my lap on top of the load was such a tight fit
that I couldn't move at all. We set off along the road following the
lakeshore. The journey seemed very long in a strange world on a bad
road. Finally we turned on a road that followed the river valley away from
the lakeshore. Water babbled in the brook as if it was singing a welcom-
ing song, pleased that people were coming to keep it company in the
heartland. Finally we started up a steep hill away from the river. When
we reached the top of the high hill, the horses were stopped and my husband started unloading the cart. I thought we had arrived but we weren't
even close.

The cow had been walking behind us tied to the cart. My husband
started walking the cow towards its new home. I stayed with the children
on top of the hill waiting for him to come back for us and the most essential things. After I had waited for what I thought was a sufficiently long
time I started to get bored. The children were getting hungry, so I dug in
the food sack for something to give them. I was beginning to worry because most of the day was gone and he still hadn't returned. Had he had
an accident? After waiting for a little longer I started to sweat out of fear
and anxiety. I couldn't start screaming because it would have alarmed the
children for fear that we were lost. Finally I heard rustling in the forest.
My husband came to us all out of breath and said: So this is where you
are? This isn't the place I left you. He had been looking for us for hours.
Now we had one more mile to go. That we had to travel by foot carrying
our belongings. The man with the horses had returned to town after the
cart had been unloaded.

I dug out a little baby carriage from amongst our things. In it I put
the coffee pot, coffee, sugar and milk. The oldest girl, Jenny, was assigned
to push this very important load. Our four-year-old son carried the bread
bag on his back. My husband and I each carried a child and as much
stuff as we could possibly carry. That's how we lumbered through the forest towards the tar paper cabin waiting for its inhabitants.

Having walked along a winding path we came upon an old railroad.

My husband said that he would walk ahead faster. A little further we were supposed to encounter the cow, and from there we ought to see the roof of the cabin. The children were getting tired from the long journey and started to get restless. Finally we arrived at the cabin. This was, then, our new home. But even though we were a few yards from the "house" we still weren't at the door. There were fallen trees and logs in front of us over which we had to jump with the children and the belongings. We managed to get the cow into the yard by going around even the slightest obstacle since cows aren't known for being high jumpers. The inside of the cabin was, of course, filled with all kinds of wood and boards just as it had been left by the hurried builder. Doors were not yet installed, nor the stove, but I really wanted that first cup of coffee in my new home. It wasn't long until the stove was installed and coffee brewed. That cup of coffee I will never forget as long as I live.

Then we had to hurry and carry all the things inside to get them away from the forest animals for the night. The cabin filled with so many things that it looked like we had much more worldly goods as necessary. And it was a good thing that we got all our rain-sensitive possessions inside because the next day it rained and snowed. We had a shortage of chairs but we got by because the bottom logs of the cabin were so big that they could be used as seats. The downside of sitting on them was, however, that so much water came in between the logs that it wasn't a good idea to sit next to the wall. We fixed the leaking wall by nailing rag rugs to the wall so that the water couldn't get straight in.

Midsummer was approaching. We had already received a message that visitors from Minnesota were coming. Therefore I had to get the place in order — to the extent that it was possible for I couldn't wax the floor or paper the walls. The expected guests were Mr. and Mrs. Kykyri. On the day appointed we were waiting for the guests and when I saw them coming, I went outside to meet them in the yard as is proper and reasonable. When Lisi saw my home and me, she started to cry and with pity in her voice she said: Oh, how did you end up in a place like this! I assured her that I hadn't cried even once yet and that I had no serious intention of starting to bemoan my fate. I told her: It's good to live here. I've never had it better anywhere. God will look after us.

— But do you really plan to stay here, Lisi asked.

— Of course, I replied. We already paid $100 for the land and

we've done a lot of work. This is like living in paradise. Look, how everything is white with blooms. Whichever way you look, life is smiling and
blooming.

In the evening the guests started looking for a place to sleep. First
they glanced at the two beds and each other. Finally the visiting matron
asked: Where are we going to sleep tonight since there are only two beds
and there are twelve of us? I assured her that there was enough room; if
we laid down sideways we could fit six to a bed.

Towards morning Kykyri jumped out of bed at the speed of lightning and asked what large, terrible animal might there be behind the
wall. In the night I had to explain to the guest that we were already
wealthy enough to own a horse. Although we only paid ten dollars for it,
it was capable of more than just waking up guests. And during that dis-
cussion in the night we told them that we also had a pig and that we were
going to buy another cow for the winter if we could rustle up enough
money and hay.

On June 10, the Kykyris left for their home in Minnesota. With bids
of God's peace and love we parted from each other. We had had many
days of fun but after the guests left there was even more work to do in the
house.

We had decided to buy a cow if we could come up with the money
and hay. One morning our neighbor, Matti Heikkilä came to tell us that
some distance away in the forest there was another river with a campsite
by it where you could make hay. So we decided to go and cut the hay for
the coming winter.

One morning I gathered bag lunches to put on the children's backs
and rakes and scythes in their hands. Carrying the smallest ones we set
out for the fields in the woods. The Heikkiläs did the same. In a few days
both families had a sizable haystack in the wilderness.

At lunch time one day talk drifted towards church matters. We all
agreed that we should get a minister to visit the area. The Heikkiläs had
a two-week-old child that needed to be baptized. So we wrote to Pastor
Wuori and invited him to visit the Washburn wilderness. He replied immediately promising to come.

A few days later, Mrs. Heikkilä was visiting us. She hadn't been there
long when one of the children brought word that two ministers had arrived. My neighbor and I went to see who the other minister was. As we
opened the door to the Heikkiläs' cabin we saw Pastor Wuori standing at

the stove stirring milk in a pot joking that he was making the other minister some 'velli' [a mixture of boiled milk and flour]. The other minister was Mr. J. F. Jackson, from Iron Belt, Wisc. waiting for the 'velli' with a smile on his lips.

The visitors, however, didn't have a lot of time to tarry. They still had a long walk back to the station to make the six o'clock train. Although we had a horse we had no carriage so we could not offer them a ride. After the baptism they hurried away but promised to visit my cabin too on their way back. Pastor Wuori stopped in the yard and looked at the small haystacks. Finally he asked: "Why did you make three stacks out of the hay? There's hardly enough hay for one." Standing up for myself I explained that while my husband was working at the quarry on the shores of Lake Superior, I cut the hay between saplings using a scythe where I could but where it was too big I used a sickle. I wasn't able to make a big haystack by myself. He finally understood why the hay was divided into three stacks. He said: "You are brave to have made your home here. May God bless you and yours. May God be with you. Stay under His wing." — And so the rare visitors departed.

Dark clouds were gathering in the sky of our lives. Until now everything had been easy going. First my husband came home one night and said there was no more work. We had enough money to buy a cow, though. That night he said that the following morning he would go find us a cow.

The next morning he went to look at the horse first. Soon he returned saying that the horse had broken his leg and that he had no choice but to shoot him. So he shot him before he set out to buy the cow. A slim consolation was he wasn't much of a horse to begin with and this way the hay would last longer. But a horse was extremely useful and you can't buy one that can walk for ten dollars.

My husband returned the next evening with a pregnant cow. The cow gave birth to a calf and died the next day. And the day after our pig died. It seemed that we would have nothing to eat during the coming winter. I wondered if God had sent us here to suffer. My husband encouraged me saying: "Don't doubt, we are only being tested. We'll have a cow for the winter."

After a while the men, Niemistö, Pakkala, Heikkilä, and Lempiälä, got work for one week. Meanwhile we women decided to turn the cow barn into a sauna since we had no cow to put in there. So we started to work — carrying rocks for the stove, making benches and pulling leaves off of tree branches for the floor. When the men were on their way back we started a fire in the stove using heavily smoking wood so that they would see from afar that there was a sauna in the village. That same night we happily bathed in the sauna.

I had forgotten all about the burials of the horse and the cow and the pig. Coming out of the sauna Lempiälä peered into the cabin and said: Couldn't we have some coffee now? I promised we'd each have two full cups of coffee that night.

I consider myself lucky to be able to reminisce about bygone times from the book of memories. For that I thank God with speech and song. Many of my erstwhile friends are already sleeping their eternal slumber.

At the end of November a butcher wanted some land cleared. He promised to give a cow as pay for clearing three acres of land and burning the sticks. Now it's done, said my husband one night upon returning home. However, the sticks hadn't been burned yet and we couldn't get the cow until it was done. In the morning we got up with this task in mind but it was snowing and the ground was under a heavy blanket of snow. The task now seemed impossible; should probably leave it until spring. My husband piled the sticks in a different way shaking away most of the snow, and so we got the cow for the winter. We also got a new horse. But how could we get another room so we could get everything under the same roof? My husband assured me that it could be done. "I'll go and hew some of those fallen pine trees and get some tar paper for the roof. Out there by the river there are some old oak boards that would make a nice floor." One day he asked me to help him pull the floor boards to the top of the hill because the hill was so steep that the horse wasn't able to do it. And so we managed to get the new room ready for Christmas.

The winter was beautiful. With some wistfulness I longed for spring. I knew the time of my convalescence was approaching and there were no doctors around. On May 17th I woke up with labor pains. Oh, dear heavenly God, please be with me! I felt as if the glow of the rising sun and its bright rays were saying: Be safe! I take care of the sick and help the suffering. For the final push I was all alone. I asked for the baby to be put on the mother's breast. The help of the Father in heaven and here on earth was much appreciated. Now I can't remember the pain for the joy. That day I asked the heavenly Father for courage so that I could relieve the pain and suffering of the sick.

On the 11th of August my husband suddenly said he was going to Dakota the next day with Pakkala, Heikkilä, Lempiälä and Lehto. It felt terrible when the men left. Only Mattson stayed. It was hot and dry. We waited for rain. We wives got together to gripe. Some dark clouds were gathering and thunder rumbling. I suggested we all go to my house. Mrs. Lempiälä came with me, the others said they'd follow shortly. For a moment we stayed in the main room. Then I suggested we go into the outbuilding. I had never taken a guest there. The weather got worse. It was pouring with rain and thunder and lightning everywhere. This lasted for about half an hour. When I opened the door, what a sight! The lid of a chest was open with clothes strewn on the floor, mixed with books that had fallen from the shelves. Now I understood why were directed to the outbuilding. It was God's voice. Lempiälä's cabin was destroyed the same way. What are we supposed to do now with no roof over our heads? I collected the wet clothes and dishes and all four families went to spend the night at the Lehto house. Nobody felt like sleeping that night and there wasn't any room to sleep anyway because there was only the one small room. In the morning I asked Mattson to put together a roof over the other room out of boards and tar paper. At least it would provide shelter from the sun if not water. I gathered all our stuff there. I spent the days there with the children, the nights were spent wherever I could find space.

My husband had taken away the horse so I wouldn't have to take care of him while he was gone. One day someone came to tell me that some other horses had kicked him in the leg and told me to take him away. We brought him home but there was nothing I could do for him; he had a huge open wound in his leg and the leg was yellow all the way down. I asked the other wives to collect all their night water. I got some oak bark to boil in it. I tied some rags at the end of a stick and washed the horse's leg with this mixture several times a day until it healed.

I ardently waited for a letter from my husband so I could tell him what had happened. He hadn't received my first letter, only the next one, and returned home right away to cut some logs for the house. It was already the end of September and we had to have a room. Against all odds it happened. It only had a rough floor and a ceiling made out of paper. In that room we lived until the following fall. Then a hail storm broke all the windows on the south side, and the roof leaked so badly that the ceiling fell down. So then we built a new ceiling out of boards and put in a new floor and chimney. But it wasn't even finished yet when we started to see the glow of the forest fires.

The beginning of October was hot and dry. Fires were raging in the forests of the region threatening the cabins of the pioneers. One day a German farmer came to urge us to leave or burn. He invited all five families to his house and said to bring all the animals as well. Immediately we carried all the dishes and clothes into a dry well and covered it carefully. Then we left for safer ground. The men stayed behind to guard the fire. Those days cries of alarm were heard from everyone's lips. A thick smoke rose into the sky with the fire licking the dry ground and burning everything on it. Fearing for the men's lives we climbed on top of a high hill and peered through binoculars to see if the houses were still standing and the men moving around.

On the third day Heikkilä came to say that the men were alive and the houses hadn't burned. On the fifth day we were able to return home. There we saw a miraculous sight for the fire had circled the houses but hadn't burned them. And even greater was our astonishment to see the haystacks still standing on the burnt-over clearing. Many people came to wonder how it was possible that the haystacks and the buildings didn't burn. God works in mysterious ways.

Everyone happily got back to work. The modest cabins felt dear to us and everyone smiled with satisfaction. I have often thought that those that never encounter any adversity do not know what joy is.

The next winter was cold and stormy. The children were all right, however, for I dressed them warmly at night and put all five sideways in the bed and covered them carefully. I remember one night standing by their bed and thanking God for entrusting me with this task of raising and safeguarding these children created by God for there is no job under the sun worthier than raising children.

The winter passed quickly and the mild spring sun melted the frost from the ground and the memories of the cold winter out of our minds. The men returned home from the winter's work to start the summer work. As early as summer we started to worry about the coming fall when the children would have to start school but we didn't know how to get clothes for them.

One day as Mrs. Heikkilä was visiting I suggested we go pick blackberries and sell them in town for there was a demand for them. The next day we went berry picking and filled large buckets with berries. The day after we went to town a bucket full of berries in one hand and a butter crock in the other. On the way we had to cross a river with no bridge. I wondered about crossing the river for I had never mastered log walking. Mrs. Heikkilä and Mrs. Lehto went first and even carried my berries. I still had the butter crock in my hand. After I'd walked a little way I started feeling as if the forest was moving up river in my eyes. I took the butter crock wrapped in rags in my teeth and crawled the length of the log. My friends were laughing out loud on the opposite bank. I felt like laughing too but couldn't because if I had opened my mouth the butter crock would have fallen to the bottom of the river.

Upon reaching town we quickly sold the berries for 10 cents a quart. We also sold the butter. With the money in hand we went to the store that sold fabric. They had thin cotton for five cents a yard and thick cotton for six cents a yard. We each bought twenty-four yards of fabric with the money from the berries and food with the butter money and returned home. We repeated these berry trips to town as long as the berry season lasted. After it ended we had plenty of fabric of all kinds.

Now that we had the fabric we had to start sewing clothes for the children: pants, shirts, dresses, and everything else they needed. When school started the children had decent clothes although at summer time it had seemed that they wouldn't be able to go school for lack of clothing.

That fall there was happiness in our lowly cabins because we didn't lack anything that would make life miserable. God himself forges us with tribulations but saves us just in time so that we would acknowledge His help and thank Him. Although our life in the wilderness was simple and we only had the bare necessities of life, life was, however, enjoyable, for joy is not in the plentitude of possessions but in the state of mind.

In the course of the years we encountered much sorrow and grief because of the children. The Lord took some of them away before I would have let them go. In 1920 our one-month-old son became ill with convulsions [most likely the cause was ergot poisoning, a fungus that infects rye]. The disease was severe and it was heart-wrenching to watch the child in great pain. Many times I asked in my mind: "Oh, God, why does this child have to suffer such pain? Is he suffering because of the sins of his fathers?" God is always right and He took little Engelbert to the joys of heaven although after much pain.

Soon afterwards our 15-year-old daughter became ill. As the years had passed some of the children had started to be at an age when they were a real help. The girl also got severe convulsions, and finally the disease got so severe that she had to be held down in bed. Many times I prayed God not to take my beloved Jenny. I said as Jacob had said that I won't let you go until you bless my beloved ones. One morning I went out to do my chores. I went down on my knees in front of God's face and prayed: "Thy will be done, Father, but relieve my sorrow and comfort me in my pain." When I ran out of words, I jumped up and went in with a happy mind assuring: "She'll get better, she'll get better, thank God." It was the morning of a day of tribulations because the disease kept getting worse although I had received an assurance through prayer that the girl would get well. All day my heart overflowed with the words: "She'll get better," although it looked like she was going to die for sure. By night fall I felt like a callous mother. But when despair is at its greatest, help is near. The girl started to get better for upon wakening she asked for something to eat. You cannot describe the feeling of gratitude I felt in my heart.

But this gratitude didn't last long for not long afterwards our youngest child became restless and you could clearly see that he was not well. I decided to take him to the doctor before the disease had a chance to progress. I got dressed and got the child ready. I picked him up to put him into the carriage. I went stiff with dread when I felt that the child was rigid. We started to massage and bathe the child but nothing helped. He breathed for another half an hour and then he went to Jesus. Many times in my mind I chided God for allowing the first one to suffer too much but taking this one too soon....

Adversity and trouble are never absent from people's lives. But neither do they always come in the same form or in daytime. They also creep in the darkness of the night. I will always remember the night of January 12, 1926. It was a beautiful evening and it was raining although it was the middle of winter. My husband was away with the horses lumberjacking. I settled down for the night with the children around 9 o'clock. While lying down we read prayers out of the long catechism brought from Finland. I didn't get undressed for I still had to go to the barn in the night.

Between three and four in the morning I awoke and heard some rustling. In the muddled state of sleep I didn't at first understand what the sound was. At first I thought it was the rain but soon thereafter I noticed a strange light outside. Our son jumped up in his bed in the loft and screamed: "Mother, the house in on fire!" I was so frightened I couldn't even reply. He came running down to see if we had burned already, in case the fire had started in our room. I was so frightened that whatever I picked up in my hand I couldn't hold on to. The children managed to take some things out of the burning house. For some unknown reason I was so distressed I tried to go back to the loft. I had gone up a few steps when I heard a voice from there: "Help me out of here!" My son had gone back to get his clothes and was suffocating from the smoke. He would surely have burned up if I hadn't gone to help. Everything in the house burned: clothes, food, furniture, everything we had. We stood outside in our night clothes in the January night warming ourselves at the flames of our home until morning.

I wasn't sad, however, for we were all grateful that we hadn't been burned. Our eight-year-old son complained that his feet were cold but I took him into the barn. Even after many years I couldn't help thinking about the sweaters I had knitted for each member of the family for which I had painstakingly spun the yarn.

In the morning I gazed at the smoking site of the house and beyond it the oak trees in their winter bareness. I comforted myself with the thought that God will clothe us as He clothes you when the spring sun thaws the frost.

I decided to write a letter to Dr. and Mrs. Koski in Hurley explaining how our house had burned down and all the clothes with it for I knew them to be good-hearted people. About the same time our son visited them in their home for he had been away and didn't know about the calamity that had befallen us. Mrs. Koski at once gathered a sackful of clothes and sent them along with our son. I was very grateful for the gift and I thanked Him who bestows all gifts for opening their hearts even wider. After a few months I received a letter from Dr. Koski in which he advised us to get a truck and come pick up some furniture. When we arrived our eyes opened wide at the sight of a dozen chairs, several tables and beds, a couch, laundry equipment and other household items from spoons to needles. And all these were bestowed to us. With my mortal tongue I couldn't quite express the gratitude in my heart. But God will reward all good deeds.

There are a lot of stories to tell from the journey of my life but most of the events would be mundane to my readers for the majority of them have traveled the same road as I have, that is, they came from Finland to America as immigrants. We may thank God for all the good that He has given us. Life is never without adversity but particularly in recent years there has been less hardship here than in our old country.

SELECTED BIBLIOGRAPHY
AND FOR FURTHER READING

Hoglund, A. William. *Finnish Immigrants in America, 1880–1920.* Madison: University of Wisconsin Press, 1960.

Jutikkala, Eino and Kauko Pirinen. *A History of Finland.* Translated by Paul Sjoblom. New York: Praeger Publishers, 1974.

Kolehmainen, John I. *The Finns in America: A Bibliographical Guide to Their History.* Hancock, MI: Finnish American Historical Library, Suomi College, 1947.

Kolehmainen, John I. and George W. Hill. *Haven in the Woods: The Story of the Finns in Wisconsin.* Madison: State Historical Society of Wisconsin, 1951 and 1965.

Racz, Istvan. *Treasures of Finnish Folk Art.* New York: Praeger Publishers, 1969.

INDEX

Page numbers referencing photos or illustrations are in *italic* type.

66

INDEX

fires, 27, 58, 60–61
fishing, 6, 14–15
Florence (Wisconsin), *17*
food, *See* diet

G.F. Sanborn Company, 24
Germantown (Wisconsin), *36*
Getto, Henry, 36

Hame, 11
Hancock (Michigan), 33
Hanko, 11, *16*
Hankoniemi, 43
Havukainen (Pastor), 50
health, 28–29, 34–35
Heikkilä, Matti, 51, 54, 55, 58
Helsinki, 9
Herbster (Wisconsin), 14
Hibbing (Minnesota), 32
holidays, 34
housing, 25–28, *37*
    construction, 5, 25–26, *36*
    See also farmsteads
Hurley, 13, 32, *41*

Industrial Workers of the World
    (IWW), 14, 33
Iron Belt (Wisconsin), 13, 31, 32, 33
Iron County (Wisconsin), 13
Iron River (Wisconsin), 33
Ironwood (Michigan), 43, 45–46

Jackson, J. F., 55
Jacobson family, 50
journalism, *See* newspapers
Juhannus, 34

Kasurinen, Henry Cass, 42
Kause, Jooperi and Kalle, 46
Kaustinen, 43
Kenosha, 9, 14, 32
Kivi (Pastor), 46–47
Kokkola, 43
Koski, Dr. and Mrs., 61
Köyhäjoki, 43
Krohn, (Pastor), 49
Kropotkin, Peter, 8

Kuopio, 11
Kuusisto, Matti, 46
Kykyri, Lisi, 46, 53

labor movement, 14, 32–33, 42
Laestadius, Lars Levi, 32
land ownership, 7, 23–24
Lapatossu, 33
Laukki, Leo, 33
Lehto family, 57, 59
Lempiälä family, 55
Little Finland Cabins, *41*
livestock, 29–30, 35, 54, 55
log cabins, 5, *21*, 25–26, *36*, *37*
logging, 9, 15, *18–20*, 22–23

map, *4*
Maple (Wisconsin), 31, 32, 33, *39*
Marinette County, 13
Marquette (Michigan), 14
Mattson family, 57
May Day, *See* Vappu
Michigan, 6, 12, 13, 33
Midsummer, *See* Juhannus
Mikkeli, 11
military, 9–10
Milwaukee, 14, 32–33
mining, 13, *17*
Mining Emigrant Association, 6
Minnesota, 12, 13, 33
Montreal (Wisconsin), 13

name changes, 31
newspapers, 33, *42*
Nieminen, John, *18*
Niemistö, Emanuel, 47
Niemistö, John, 24, 37, 47
Niemistö, Kristiina, 16
    memoir of, 43–61
North York (Wisconsin), 31

Oulu (Finland), 6, 11, 14
Oulu (Wisconsin), 33, *36*, 41
Owen (Wisconsin), 23, 31

Pakkala, Matti, 51, 55
Pelto ja Koti, 33

THE AUTHOR

MARK KNIPPING has a master's degree in American History from the University of Wisconsin–Madison. He joined the staff of the Wisconsin Historical Society in 1971 as the Chief of Research and Interpretation at Old World Wisconsin and assisted in the planning and developing of that historic site. He has also researched and managed other historic sites, such as Pendarvis and the Herrling Sawmill. Since his retirement in 2004, Mr. Knipping continues to pursue his research interests, such as the historic pottery of the Sheboygan, Wisconsin, area and serves as a consultant to museums.